CW00550885

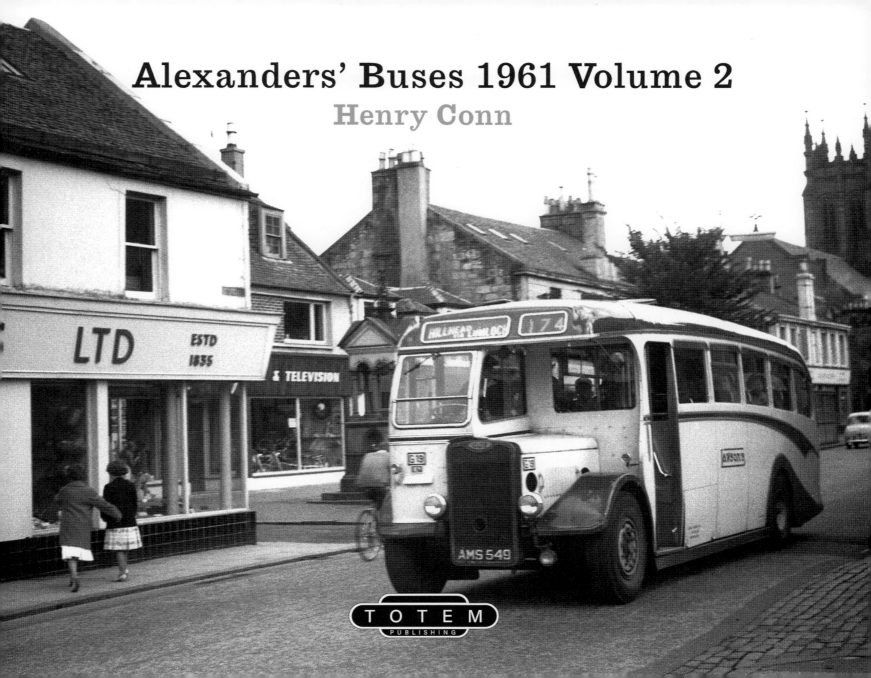

Alexanders' Buses 1961 Volume 2

Henry Conn

TOTEM
PUBLISHING

Front Cover view. On Seagate on 30 August on the north side of Seagate bus station in Dundee is R334, (WG 9724), an all Leyland TD7 new in June 1942; R334 and R335 were the last Leyland TD7s delivered new to Alexanders and the bodywork of both was supplied by Leyland in shell form and finished by Alexander.

Back cover view. On Marshall Place with the South Inch to the right of the view, turning into Scott Street in Perth is RO720, (GYL 449), an NCME bodied Guy Arab II new to London Transport in March 1946. Acquired by Alexander in March 1953 RO720 ran for Alexander in the all red livery of the Perth City fleet. This view was taken on 21 October and RO720 is working the town service between Friarton and Muirton North.

Frontis Image. (1) Working an ex-David Lawson service to Hillhead via Lumloch from Glasgow on 27 August is G19, (AMS 549), a Duple coach bodied Guy Arab III new to David Lawson in March 1947; G19 would be sold to Highland Omnibuses in May 1965 as their K33 and would be withdrawn by the end of 1965.

Introduction

As in the previous volume, rather than write about the history of Alexanders, which has been covered by a number of books, I will cover headlines and stories that made the headlines in the UK and from throughout the world that the time period of this book covers.

The premiere of the film *Victim* on 31 August was notable as the first in English to use the word "homosexual". A couple of days later the first Mothercare shop opens, as Mother-and-Child Centre in Kingston upon Thames. The film *A Taste of Honey*, including themes of interracial relationship, unmarried pregnancy and homosexuality, is released on 14 September. Two days later three people die and 35 are injured when a stand collapses during a Glasgow Rangers football match at Ibrox Park. On 17 September police arrest over 1,300 protesters in Trafalgar Square during a CND rally. Europe's first 'moving pavement', now known as a travolator, debuts at Bank station on the London Underground on 27 September.

On October 1 religious programme *Songs of Praise* is first broadcast on BBC Television and it will still be running fifty years later. At the same time Acker Bilk's haunting *Stranger on the Shore* is released. Eight days later, Skelmersdale, a small Lancashire town fifteen miles north-east of Liverpool, is designated as a new town and its population will expand over the coming years, bolstered by large council housing developments to rehouse families from inner city slums on Merseyside. A volcanic eruption on the South Atlantic British overseas territory of Tristan da Cunha on 10 October causes the island's entire population to be evacuated to Surrey, where they will remain until 1963. The first edition of *Private Eye*, the satirical magazine, is published in London on 25 October.

On November 2 Penguin Books is cleared of obscenity for publishing D.H. Lawrence's *Lady Chatterley's Lover* after a heavily publicised trial at the Old Bailey, London. The success of the trial made it a landmark case in British obscenity law, significantly affecting the publishing world, which was now given more freedom to launch books with explicit content. The uncensored version of *Lady Chatterley's Lover* goes on sale in the UK in November and all 200,000 published copies are sold out after just one day.

This book is a picture album (not intended to be a history of the company), and features views from the period between 27 August and 26 November and features views in chronological order taken in Kirkintilloch, Kilsyth, Larbert, Leven, St Andrews, Dundee, Falkirk, Perth, Stirling, Bannockburn, Lochgelly and Cowdenbeath. All the views in each volume are unpublished. Enjoy the nostalgia, and please forward any comments or thoughts to me. I look forward to reading them.

Henry Conn
September 2021

Acknowledgements

Without kind permission from Robin Fell for access to the wonderful collection of Alexander buses and coaches negatives from 1961 this book would not have been possible, my sincere thanks.

2. (Left) On the same day, working an ex-David Lawson service between Blanefield and Chryston, is P335, (WG 4449), originally an Alexander coach bodied Leyland TS7 new in January 1937; P335 received a new Alexander coach body in 1949 and it was converted to bus seating in 1959. This bus was in the Lawson fleet between 1949 until the split in May 1961 and was later sold to McCulloch of Bishopbriggs in November 1964.

3. (Above) In Kirkintilloch on 27 August is P645, (WG 9335), an Alexander bodied Leyland TS8 delivered to the David Lawson fleet in May 1940; P645 has received the legal lettering of Alexanders and is freshly re-painted from the Lawson livery. The bus would be sold in May 1963.

4. Still in Lawsons livery and still with David Lawson legal lettering, this is P679, (WG 9515), an Alexander bodied Leyland TS8 new in December 1940; P679 is working the Waterside to Glasgow service via Balmore and this view, taken on 27 August, may be the last of the bus in service as it was scrapped by Alexander Midland in September.

5. At Kilsyth depot in Edward Street on 27 August is P684, (WG 9754), a Willowbrook bodied Leyland TS11 new in August 1942. The Leyland TS11 was a rare bus and when Leyland turned their entire resources over to war work the final twenty-two chassis emerged in mid-1942; P684 passed to a showman in October 1964 and was purchased for preservation in March 1971.

6. (Left) The next two views were also taken at Kilsyth depot on 27 August. Indicating route 1C between Kilsyth (Hamill Drive) and Glasgow via Twechar Bridge with a journey time of around 45 minutes this is A73, (BMS 107), a Burlingham bodied AEC Regal new in October 1947; A73 passed to a showman in July 1965.

7. (Right) Route 1 was the regular 40 minute service between Kilsyth and Glasgow, Dundas Street, via Kirkintilloch and Bishopbriggs. Regular performers on this service in 1961 were Alexander bodied Leyland PD1s like RA42, (BWG 87), new in July 1948; RA42 would be sold for scrap, minus engine, in October 1968.

8. The next day we are in Leven and this is P603, an Alexander bodied Leyland TS8 special new in March 1940; note that Visocchi's fresh ice cream was considered to be one of the best in Scotland.

9. We have travelled thirteen miles from Leven to St Andrews and parked outside the depot on 28 August is G26, (AMS 566), a Duple bodied Guy Arab III new in March 1947; G22 had originally operated for David Lawson from new and passed to Alexanders in 1953. A service provided by St Andrews depot during the summer months was to Craigtoun, a country park located approximately 4 miles to the south-west of St Andrews in the county of Fife, Scotland. The park was originally part of the Mount Melville Estate, 47 acres of which was purchased by Fife County Council for £25,000 in 1947.

10. A total of 101 Guy Arab III single deckers were purchased between 1946 and 1948, numbered G1 to G101 (AMS 531-580, AWG 565-574, BMS 595, BMS 584-593 and BMS 842-871), and all delivered with 5LW engines. The first 71 were coaches, with various body manufacturers, and the last 30 were buses, bodied by Guy. Twenty of the coaches received Massey bodies, in two batches, one in 1946 and one in 1948, and G34, (AMS 564), is one of the 1946 batch. These examples arrived in Bluebird livery, but many were modified for bus use in the late 1950s.

11. In the forecourt of St Andrews depot posing for the camera on 28 August is PB7, (DMS 820), one of the ten Alexander coach bodied Leyland OPS2/1s all new in December 1951 which were transferred to Alexander Fife on 15 May; PB7 was sold in 1970 and is currently in preservation.

12. An interesting contrast at St Andrews on 28 August with a twelve year difference in age between PD111, (KMS 480), an Alexander bodied Leyland PSUC1/2 new in March 1958, and G36, (AMS 566), a Massey bodied Guy Arab III new in July 1946.

13. The next five views were all taken on 28 August and seen here at the St Andrews bus station adjacent to the depot is PD200, (OMS 276), an Alexander coach bodied Leyland PSUC1/2 new in October 1960. Route 23 was between St Andrews and Glasgow via Cupar, Milnathort and Stirling with a journey time of three and a half hours.

14. (Left) In the parking area at St Andrews depot are PA52, (BMS 214), an Alexander coach bodied Leyland PS1 new in March 1948, PA26, another Alexander coach bodied Leyland PS1 new in May 1947, and the curvaceous G36, (AMS 566), a Massey bodied Guy Arab III new in July 1946; PA52 would be the last in service and would be sold to Lendrick Muir school in August 1969.

15. (Above) This is Kelty based PD121, (KMS 490), an Alexander coach bodied Leyland PSUC1/2 which entered service in May 1959; PD121 will be departing from St Andrews bus stance to Dunfermline via Cupar, Milnathort and Kelty, a journey of just under two hours.

16. (Top Left) With St Andrews in the background this is Anstruther based PD69, (GWG 295), an Alexander bodied Leyland PSUC1/2 on route 355 to Leven; PD69 would have left Newport on the Tay Estuary just over 45 minutes before this view was taken. It will take another one and half hours to reach Leven via all the lovely coastal villages and towns along the south Fife coast such as Crail, Anstruther, Pittenweem, St Monance and Elie.

17. (Bottom Left) An hour later, also working route 355 between Newport and Leven, this is Anstruther based PD68, (GWG 294), also an Alexander bodied Leyland PSUC1/2, both were new in November 1955. Nearing the end of its journey, around one and a quarter hours after this view was taken, PD68 will be stopping in Kilconquhar, a village well known to me as it is where my brother's wedding took place many moons ago; another half an hour from Kilconquhar, PD68 will reach Leven.

18. (Above) All the Dundee views that follow were taken on 31 August. Standing against the Dundee depot wall is A9, (AMS 589), a Burlingham bodied AEC Regal new in August 1946. Alexander was not normally an AEC customer but 82 were delivered between 1946 and March 1948; the Burlingham bodied Regals served as buses only.

19. Working the very regular Dundee to Carnoustie service at Seagate is A37, an Alexander bodied AEC Regal new in August 1947; A37 passed to Aberdeen Corporation City Engineers Department in September 1967 where it remained until 1974. The van is a Royal Mail 10cwt Morris J; the Royal Mail was the single largest purchaser of the van, buying over 17,000 for their fleet.

20. Nearing the end of its service to the bus station in Dundee is PA67, (BMS 694), an Alexander coach bodied Leyland PS1 new in March 1948. The 6 ton lorry behind PA67 is a Jensen; after the war Jensen launched another lightweight lorry, the JNSN, which was easily recognisable by the radiator grille, shaped to the JNSN letters. It was available in a range of forms including lorries, trucks, pantechnicons, and even as a luxury coach. The vehicles sold well and remained in production until 1956.

21. In Dundee bus station is PA163, (CWG 205), an Alexander coach bodied Leyland PS1 new in March 1950. Also in view is Forfar based PA1, (AWG 536), an Alexander bodied Leyland PS1 new in March 1947, numerically the first PS1 to be delivered to Alexanders; the only difference that I can see between the two is the aperture for the indicator display.

22. Leaving Dundee bus station for Blairgowrie via Alyth is AC76, (GWG 480), an Alexander bodied AEC Monocoach new in July 1955; I think the missing service number would be 153 and AC76 would arrive in Blairgowrie about an hour after this view was taken.

23. Entering Dundee bus station with a healthy load
of passengers is AC92, (HMS 241), an Alexander
bodied AEC Reliance new in July 1956. The
indicator numbers have been missing in a number
of the views taken in Dundee; I think AC92 is
arriving from Brechin via Finavon on route 154.

24. (Left) This is Dock Street with tram lines still visible after nearly four years since their last use. Indicating route 19B, Dundee to Perth, but working a short ten minute journey to Invergowrie, this is AC95, (HMS 244), an Alexander bodied AEC Reliance new in July 1956.

25. (Above) Entering Dundee bus station after a near four hour journey from Glasgow via Stirling and Perth, this is Stirling based PD77, (JMS 195), an Alexander coach bodied Leyland PSUC1/2 new in September 1956.

26. Leaving Dundee on the hour long journey to Perth, Tay Street, on route 19B via Invergowrie, Longforgan, Inchture and Glencarse, this is PG78, (JMS 196), an Alexander coach bodied Leyland PSUC1/2 new in September 1956. The Dundee Corporation bus is 257, (FYJ 797), a Weymann bodied Daimler CVG6 new in 1957.

27. Looking very smart in the Bluebird livery is Stonehaven based AC109, (JWG 689), an Alexander coach bodied AEC Reliance new in June 1957. Route 11 between Aberdeen and Dundee would take over 3 hours with stops at Cammachmore, Stonehaven, Inverbervie, St Cyrus, Montrose, Inverkeilor, Arbroath, Carnoustie, Monifieth and Broughty Ferry.

28. A number of the 1958 Alexander coach bodied Albion MR11Ls transferred to the Northern fleet in May 1961; one of these is NL15, (KWG 590), new in June 1958. The withdrawal of the Albions in the Northern fleet began in 1973 and the last survived until October 1975.

29. The gentleman to the right seems to be more interested in the photographer rather than R334 about to enter Dundee bus station; R334 features on the cover of this volume and would be sold to Millburn Motors of Glasgow in September 1962 whilst on loan to Alexander Midland and would be scrapped four months later.

30. (Above) Alyth is a small town in Perth & Kinross five miles north-east of Blairgowrie. The missing service number in August 1961, I think, would be 153A between Dundee and Alyth via Aucterhouse, Newtyle and Meigle with a journey time of around fifty minutes; this is A31, (AWG 618), an Alexander coach bodied AEC Regal new in August 1947.

31. (Right) Arbroath based RA49, (BWG 94), an Alexander bodied Leyland PD1 new in July 1948, is indicating route 11 from Dundee to Arbroath via Broughty Ferry, Monifieth, Carnoustie and Muirdrum, a regular service with a journey of one hour; RA49 was exported to Boston in the USA in January 1971.

32. Arriving in Dundee from Forfar via Murroes is Forfar based PA132, (CMS 200), an Alexander coach bodied Leyland PS1 new in June 1949; the parked car is a 1960 Dundee registered Austin Cambridge A55 Mark II and the Guinness advert in the background is a new one to me.

33. Seventeen miles from Dundee is the large village of Letham; leaving Dundee bus station with a healthy passenger load for Letham is Dundee based PA152, (CWG 34), an Alexander coach bodied Leyland PS1 new in March 1950; PA152 would be sold to a farm in Inchture in April 1971.

34. Six AEC Regal IIIs were ordered by James Sutherland of Peterhead before they were taken over by Alexanders in 1950. They were to be bodied by Duple but were put to the back of the queue by Alexanders and received some of their last half cab bodies, 8 foot wide on a 7 foot 6 inch chassis. Representing the batch in Dundee bus station is A99, (DMS 125), new in May 1951.

35. As AC50, (GWG 101), is an Alexander bus bodied AEC Reliance, new in June 1955, I think that the bus is working the regular service 19B between Dundee and Tay Street in Perth. The Dundee to Glasgow service also stopped in Tay Street, Perth, but coaches were used on this longer service; AC50 passed to a Dancing Group in Chadderton in March 1975.

36. Leaving Dundee with a healthy load of passengers, this is Dundee based AC76, (GWG 480), an Alexander bodied AEC Monocoach new in July 1955. Only 188 AEC Monocoaches were built, the majority bodied by Park Royal, with Scottish operators taking delivery of 151. In the opposite direction is Dundee Corporation 280, (HTS 280), a Metro Cammell bodied Daimler CVG6 new in 1958.

37. (Above) Another Alexander bodied AEC Monocoach, this is Forfar based AC78, (GWG 482) leaving the parking area at Dundee bus station to move to its stance for service to Forfar; AC78 would take the long ferry trip to Shetland in September 1975, acquired by Leask of Lerwick, passing to Sandwick Transport in January 1976 to be used Sullom Voe oil contract work. It later moved to a drivers croft in Sumbrugh, used as a greenhouse and was noted as a storeshed in Sumbrugh in February 2014.

38. Nice to see, a bus with the correct destination screen and route number, this is AC95, an Alexander bodied AEC Reliance new in July 1956. Various poster advertisements were made to promote Senior Service cigarettes and this one is Senior Service *Everywhere*; Senior Service cigarettes were introduced in 1925 and were discontinued in the UK in January 2020.

39. Leaving Dundee for the over three hour journey to Aberdeen is AC124, (JWG 704), an Alexander coach bodied AEC Reliance new in June 1957. To the right of the view is a Bedford CA van, which were produced in Luton between 1952 and 1969.

40. Arriving at Dundee bus station after a forty minute journey from Carnoustie is RB204, (KWG 665), an Alexander bodied Leyland PD3/3 new in August 1958. UK construction and use regulations were further relaxed in July 1956, with the maximum double-deck length on two axles being increased to 30 foot and gross vehicle weight to 14 tons. Leyland immediately responded to these relaxed regulations by announcing a new six-model range of PD3s with 18 foot 3 inch wheelbases, all for 8 foot wide bodies. The PD3/3 variant had a synchromesh gear box, vacuum brakes and a full-width bonnet; Alexander took batches with 67-seat lowbridge bodies until 1961.

41. This is R335, (WG 9725), an all Leyland TD7 new in July 1942, and is viewed here working a short route 11C between Dundee and Monifieth, a journey of around twenty-five minutes. At over nineteen years old at the time of this view, R335 would remain in the Alexander Northern fleet until February 1963.

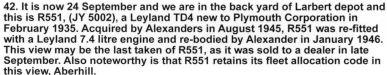

42. It is now 24 September and we are in the back yard of Larbert depot and this is R551, (JY 5002), a Leyland TD4 new to Plymouth Corporation in February 1935. Acquired by Alexanders in August 1945, R551 was re-fitted with a Leyland 7.4 litre engine and re-bodied by Alexander in January 1946. This view may be the last taken of R551, as it was sold to a dealer in late September. Also noteworthy is that R551 retains its fleet allocation code in this view, Aberhill.

43. Also standing in the Larbert yard withdrawn is R546, (JY 6732), a Leyland TD4 new to Plymouth Corporation in December 1935, acquired by Alexander in July 1945 and fitted with a new Alexander body in January 1946; R546 (note with no readable depot code) would be sold for scrap just after this view was taken. Partially visible is R429, (WG 3493), an Alexander bodied Leyland TD4 new in July 1936, originally as a single decker, receiving a new Alexander body as shown in this view in January 1944; R429 would be sold at the same time as R546.

44. In comparison to the elderly withdrawn double deck buses in the background, this is RB265, (SWG 621), an Alexander bodied Leyland PD3A/3 just three months old when this view was taken. The service indicated is 18A, the very regular Glasgow to Falkirk route via Kilsyth, Bonnybridge and Larbert.

45. (Left) Also at Larbert depot is R230, (WG 8249), an all Leyland TD5 new in February 1939; R230 would be one of the last TD5s to be withdrawn, surviving until February 1963.

46. (Above) The last view taken in Larbert on 24 September is of R330, (WG 9633), an all Leyland TD7 new in March 1942, and alongside is R315, (WG 9544), an all Leyland TD7 new in February 1941; both were sold to a scrap dealer, R330 in November 1963 and R315 in January 1964.

47. Route 90 was between Dunfermline and Falkirk via Kincardine, Culross and Cairneyhill. It would be unusual for PC51, (EMS 169), an Alexander coach bodied Leyland PSU1/15 new in April 1953, to be running this hour long journey on 25 September. The overtaking car is a locally registered Standard Ensign which were produced between 1957 and 1961; the Ensign was the first Standard to feature a four speed gearbox and the gear lever was moved from the column to the floor.

48. Leaving Falkirk on 12 October on the one hour twenty minute journey to Dundas Street, Glasgow, via Bonnybridge and Kilsyth is Kirkintilloch based EB264, (SWG 620), an Alexander bodied Leyland PD3A/3 new to Alexander Midland in August 1961. The car in the background is a 1956 Vauxhall Velox.

49. The next nine views were taken in Perth on 19 October. The first bus featured, standing outside the Alexander Midland bus depot in Riggs Road, is RO545, (AMS 8), a Weymann bodied Guy Arab II new in June 1945 which remained in the fleet until sale in August 1963.

50. (Left) Between March and May 1953 Alexander purchased one Guy Arab I and fifteen Guy Arab IIs from London Transport and all ran for Alexander in the red livery of the Perth City fleet. The first to feature on 19 October is RO698, (GYE 91), a Park Royal bodied Guy Arab II new in July 1945 and seen here working the Perth City service to Scott Street.

51. (Below) Working the Perth City service to Darnhall is RO531, (AMS 277), an NCME bodied Guy Arab II new to Alexander in December 1944; RO531 would be scrapped by Alexander Midland in August 1963.

52. Standing outside Perth City Hall is A8, (AMS 588), a Burlingham bodied AEC Regal new in August 1946; A8 would be sold to a Grangemouth contractor for staff transport in July 1964.

53. Leaving Riggs Road depot in Perth is Crieff based AC49, (GWG 100), an Alexander bodied AEC Reliance new in May 1955; the journey to its home base starting at Perth Station will take around 50 minutes via Methven and Gilmerton. Also exiting the depot to begin a local City service to Hillyland is RO528, (AMS 274), an NCME bodied Guy Arab II new in December 1944. The car in the background is a Rover 90.

54. Passing a Kirkcaldy Linoleum Market on a Perth City service to Hillyland is RO718, (GYL 437), an NCME bodied Guy Arab II new to London Transport in December 1945 and acquired by Alexander in March 1953 for Perth City Services. The car on the opposite side of the road is a post-war Austin 10 and the van is a Morris LD.

55. In service to Friarton is RO720, (GYL 449), an NCME bodied Guy Arab II new to London Transport in March 1946 and acquired by Alexander in March 1953. While many 10cwt Fordson or Thames vans were converted into passenger carriers by their owners, there was a factory-built job; known as the Estate Car and bar the windows and seating, the specification of the Estate car was identical to that of the E83W van, in that it was powered by a 10HP 1172cc side-valve engine, coupled to a three-speed gearbox. The Fordson E83W in this view is Dundee registered and new in 1947.

56. (Left) This is RO722, (HGC 135), a Park Royal bodied Guy Arab II new to London Transport in March 1946 and the last to be acquired by Alexander in May 1953. The ex-London Guy Arabs for Perth City services acquired between March and May 1953 were withdrawn between June 1962 and December 1963; my family arrived to live in Scone in Perthshire just after the Guy Arabs were withdrawn and my first memories of buses from Scone to the High Street were of Bristol LD6Gs.

57. (Right) Another view of RO722, passing a new Dundee registered Ford Anglia 105E; the Ford Anglia 105E was introduced in 1959 and with its American influenced styling was a very popular car to buy with just over a million cars produced between 1959 and 1967.

58. All the remaining views in Perth were taken on 21 October. A number of routes from and to Perth had stops in Tay Street with the River Tay to the right of this view. This is the second of the Weymann bodied Guy Arab IIs delivered in June 1945, RO544, (AMS 7), and is indicating Auchterarder as its destination, but the service number is for the Perth to Dundee service.

59. I think this is Glasgow Road and RO545, (AMS 8), the other Weymann bodied Guy Arab II new in June 1945, has just crossed the bridge over the main railway lines and is about to take the steady climb through Cherrybank with Craigie Golf Club on the left and Perth Academy on the right.

60. (Above) Standing outside a very busy Riggs Road depot is A8, (AMS 588), a Burlingham bodied AEC Regal which was photographed two days earlier in the book standing outside Perth City Hall. Exiting the depot is 181, (WG 2365), a Leyland LT5B new in 1934 and re-built to a tow wagon in 1955 and passing to Alexander Midland in May 1961.

61. (Right) Although it was numerically the final Alexander bodied Leyland PS1 to be delivered to the company, PA196, (AWG 591), had a re-issued registration number, and was new in July 1950; PA196 was withdrawn in 1969.

62. We are in the Station Square in Perth where many of the country services used this area as a terminus. The route from Perth to Blairgowrie via Guildtown, Cargill and Meikleour took around fifty minutes. This is Blairgowrie based A77, (BMS 463), a Burlingham bodied AEC Regal, new in January 1948, and will soon be re-painted to the yellow livery of Alexander Northern.

63. On Marshall Place with the lovely St Leonard's in the Fields Church in the background, and South Inch to the left of this view, this is Alexander Fife Newburgh based G78, (BMS 848), a Guy bodied Guy Arab III new in February 1948. The journey to St Andrews will take the best part of an hour and three quarters and will pass through Pitscottie, where, many years later, I stayed for a year whilst studying at Elmwood College in Cupar.

64. With the Station Hotel in Perth in the background this is PA117, (BWG 522), an Alexander coach bodied Leyland PS1 new in March 1949. The lovely journey to Aberfeldy via Luncarty, Bankfoot, Birnam, Dunkeld, Dalguise and Grandtully would take an hour and three quarters. Crieff based AC49, (GWG 100), will take about fifty minutes for its journey between Perth and Crieff.

65. Posing outside Riggs Road depot is W235, (CMS 47), a Duple coach bodied Bedford OB new in April 1949; to my mind a classic coach which survived with Alexander Midland until sold in April 1963.

66. (Left) Inside Riggs Road depot is the oldest of the Guy Arabs acquired by Alexander between March and May 1953; RO696, (GLL 566), is a Park Royal bodied Guy Arab I new to London Transport in June 1943 and at the time of this view would have less than a year's service before being sold for scrap in August 1962.

67. (Right) A good view of the Tay Street terminus with the River Tay in the background. Route 19 was the four hour long service between Dundee and Glasgow; this is PD110, (KMS 479), an Alexander coach bodied Leyland PSUC1/2 new in May 1958 which is indicating a short journey of fifty minutes from Perth to Blackford via Auchterarder. In the background working route 326 to Dunfermline via Glenfarg, Milnathort, Kinross, Kelty and Kingseat is Alexander Fife PD197, (OMS 273), an Alexander bodied Leyland PSUC1/2 new in August 1960.

68. Turning from Kings Place into St Leonards Bridge heading for Darnhall is P670, (WG 9506), an Alexander bodied Leyland TS8 new in March 1940; P670 would be scrapped by Alexander Midland in December 1962.

69. On 12 November we are now in the back yard of Larbert depot and awaiting disposal is R555, (JY 6756), new to Plymouth Corporation with a Weymann body in January and fitted with a new Alexander body in February 1946; R555 would be transferred to Alexander Northern in May 1961, may have seen some service, and was sold for scrap three months after this view was taken.

70. In this view at Larbert, R232, (WG 8251), an all Leyland TD5 new in February 1939, is still available for service and would be until April 1963. Standing alongside is out of service R554, (JY 5032), a Leyland TD4 new to Plymouth in April 1935 with an Alexander body new in 1946 which passed to Alexander Northern in May 1961; R554 would probably not have been used by Alexander Northern and passed to the Stirlingshire Police just after this view was taken.

71. Also at Larbert showing pretty horrendous upper body work damage is RB206, (NWG 895), an Alexander bodied Leyland PD3/3 new in January 1960; as RB206 was less than two years old at the time of this view it was repaired and remained with Alexander Midland until September 1975.

72. Two days later, 14 November, and we are at the busy bus station in Stirling; indicating route 14C between Clackmannan and Stirling via Alloa, Cambus and Tullibody, this is Alloa based PD83, (JMS 201), an Alexander bodied Leyland PSUC1/2 new in October 1956; journey time between Clackmannan and Stirling would be around forty minutes.

73. Also at Stirling bus station is PD146, an Alexander coach bodied Leyland PSUC1/2 new in May 1959; PD146 is working route 19 between Glasgow and Dundee and will take the best part of two and a half hours to travel to Dundee. In the background, indicating route 58 between Dunblane and Cowie, is one of the 1960 intake of ECW bodied Bristol LD6Gs.

74. In Forth Street, Stirling, this is Stirling based P657, (WG 9493), an Alexander bodied Leyland TS8 new in December 1940; P657 would be scrapped by Alexander Midland in August 1963.

75. The last views in this volume were taken on 26 November and winter has arrived early in Lochgelly. Indicating route 333 between Lochgelly, Auchterderran Road and Newport Pier, this is Alexander Fife G40, (AMS 570), a Massey coach bodied Guy Arab III new in July 1946. Alongside is GA15, (JWG 506), an Alexander coach bodied Guy Arab LUF new in May 1957.

76. Working route 314 to Dalbeath Crescent is RO479, (AMS 151), an NCME bodied Guy Arab II new in July 1944; remarkably RO479 would remain with Alexander Fife until sale in May 1968.

77. Also on a 314 to Dunfermline is RO585, (AWG 371), a Cravens bodied Guy Arab III new in January 1948; RO585 would be sold in May 1970. Cravens, of Darnall in Sheffield, had a long history of supplying bodywork for railway vehicles and buses, the last Craven bodied bus was a 1966 Bedford.

78. Another Cravens bodied Guy Arab III working route 314 to Dunfermline is RO589, (AWG 375), new in February 1948. This view clearly shows the skill achieved by the painters in the paint shop of Alexanders as side panel adverts were hand painted; having served Alexander for over twenty years RO569 was sold in November 1969.

79. At Cowdenbeath depot is RO475, (AMS 147), an NCME bodied Guy Arab II new in July 1944. Note this bus is showing another method of displaying side panel adverts, which was on an independent panel secured to the side of the bus by screws; RO475 would be withdrawn in October 1967.

80. The last view in this volume at Cowdenbeath depot is of RO640, (HGC 166), a Weymann bodied Guy Arab II new to London Transport in October 1945 and acquired by Alexander in December 1951. All of the ex-London Transport Guy Arabs were sold by mid-July 1964.